Nehemiah
Restoring The Breach

By
E. G. White

TEACH Services, Inc.
Brushton, New York

Copyright © 1997 TEACH Services, Inc.

ISBN 1-57258-124-7
Library of Congress Catalog Card No. 96-61473

Published by

TEACH Services, Inc.
RR 1, Box 182
Brushton, New York 12916

Table of Contents

Chapter 1

A Holy Purpose to Restore Jerusalem

Among the children of Israel scattered in heathen lands as a result of the seventy years' captivity, there were Christian patriots,—men who were true to principle; men who esteemed the service of God above every earthly advantage; men who would honor God at the loss of all things. These men had to suffer with the guilty; but in the providence of God their captivity was the means of bringing them to the front. Their example of untarnished integrity shines with heaven's luster

Comparatively few of the Jews in captivity took advantage of the liberal decree of Cyrus providing for their return to their own land. But those who did return began the work of rebuilding the temple and the walls of Jerusalem. This great undertaking was carried forward very slowly. Years passed, and the work was still uncompleted. Then God brought forward a man of opportunity, through whom he worked for the restoration of the city of his chosen people.

Nehemiah, a Hebrew exile, occupied a position of influence and honor in the Persian court. As cup-bearer of the king, he was familiarly admitted to the royal presence; and by virtue of this intimacy, and his own high abilities and tried fidelity, he became the monarch's counselor. Yet in that heathen land, surrounded by royal pomp and splendor, he did not forget the God of his fathers or the people who had been entrusted with the holy oracles. With deepest interest, his heart turned toward Jerusalem, and his hopes and joys were bound up with her prosperity. Days of peculiar trial and affliction had come to the chosen city. Messengers from Judah described to Nehemiah its condition. The second temple had been reared, and portions of the city rebuilt; but the work of restoration was imperiled, the temple services were disturbed, and the people were kept in constant alarm, by the fact that the walls of the city were in ruins, and the gates burned with fire. The capital of Judah was fast becoming a desolate place, and the few inhabitants remaining were daily embittered by the taunts of their idolatrous assailants, "Where is your God?"

The soul of the Hebrew patriot was overwhelmed by these evil tidings. So great was his sorrow that he could not eat or drink. He "wept and mourned certain days, and fasted." But when the first outburst of grief was over, he turned to the sure Helper. "I prayed," he said, "before the God of heaven." He knew that all this ruin had come because of the transgression of Israel; and in deep humiliation he came before God for pardon of sin and a renewal of the divine favor. He addressed his petitions to the God of heaven, "the great and terrible God;" for such the Lord had shown himself to be in the fearful judgments brought upon Israel. But with a gleam of hope, Nehemiah continued, "That keepeth covenant and mercy with them that love him and observe his commandments." For repentant and believing Israel there was still mercy.

Faithfully the man of God made confession of his sins and the sins of his people: "Let thine ear now be attentive, and thine eyes open, that thou mayest hear the prayer of thy servant, which I pray before thee now, day and night, for the children of Israel thy servants, and confess the sins of the children of Israel, which we have sinned against thee: both I and my father's house have sinned. We have dealt very corruptly against thee, and have not kept the commandments, nor the statutes, nor the judgments, which thou commandedst thy servant Moses."

And now, by faith taking fast hold of the divine promise, Nehemiah laid down at the footstool of heavenly mercy his petition that God would maintain the cause of his penitent people, restore their strength, and build up their waste places. God had been faithful to his threatenings when his people separated from him; he had scattered them abroad among the nations, according to his word. And Nehemiah found in this very fact an assurance that he would be equally faithful in fulfilling his promises. His people had now returned in penitence and faith to keep his commandments: and God himself had said that if they would do this, even though they were cast out into the uttermost part of the earth, he would gather them thence, and would cause the light of his countenance again to shine upon them. This promise had been given more than a thousand years before; but through all the centuries it stood unchanged. God's word can not fail.

Nehemiah's faith and courage strengthened as he grasped the promise. His mouth was filled with holy arguments. He pointed to the dishonor that would be cast upon God, were his people, now that they had returned to him, to be left in weakness and oppression.

Nehemiah had often poured out his soul thus before God in behalf of his people. And as he prayed, a holy purpose had been forming in his mind, that if he could obtain the consent of the king, and the necessary aid in procuring implements and material, he would himself undertake the arduous task of rebuilding the walls of Jerusalem, and seeking to restore the national strength. And now, in closing his prayer, he entreated the Lord to grant him favor in the sight of the king, that this cherished plan might be carried out.

—Southern Watchman, March 1, 1904

Chapter 2

Prevailing Prayer

Four months Nehemiah was compelled to wait for a favorable opportunity to present his request to the king. During this period, while his heart was oppressed with grief, he constantly endeavored to carry a cheerful and happy countenance. In his seasons of retirement, many were the prayers, the penitential confessions, and the tears of anguish, witnessed by God and angels; but all this was concealed from human sight. The regulations of

Eastern courts forbade any manifestation of sorrow within them. All must appear gay and happy in those halls of luxury and splendor. The distress without was not to cast its shadow in the presence of royalty.

But at last the sorrow that burdened Nehemiah's heart could no longer be concealed. Sleepless nights devoted to earnest prayer, care-filled days, dark with the shadow of hope deferred, left their trace upon his countenance. The keen eye of the monarch, jealous to guard his own safety, was accustomed to read countenances and penetrate disguises. Seeing that some secret trouble was preying upon his servant, he suddenly inquired, "Why is thy countenance sad, seeing thou art not sick? This is nothing else but sorrow of heart."

This question filled the listener with apprehension. Would not the king be angry to hear that while outwardly engaged in his service, the courtier's thoughts had been far away with his afflicted people? Would not the offender's life be forfeited? And his cherished plan for restoring the strength of Jerusalem—was it not about to be overthrown? "Then," he said, "I was very sore afraid." With trembling lips and tearful eyes he revealed the cause of his sorrow,—the city, which was the place of his fathers' sepulchers, lying waste, and its gates consumed with fire. The touching recital awakened the sympathy of the monarch without arousing his idolatrous prejudices; another question gave the opportunity which Nehemiah had long sought: "For what dost thou make request?" But the man of God did not venture to reply until he had first sought direction from One higher than Artaxerxes. "I prayed," he said, "to the God of heaven."

Nehemiah felt that he had a sacred trust which required help from the king, and that everything depended upon addressing him in a right manner. In that brief prayer, Nehemiah pressed into the presence of the King of kings, and enlisted on his side a power that can turn hearts as the rivers of water are turned.

A precious lesson is this for all Christians. Whenever we are brought into difficulty or danger, even when surrounded by those who do not love or fear God, the heart may send up its cry for help, and there is One who has pledged himself to come to our aid. This is the kind of prayer Christ meant when he said, "Pray without ceasing." We are not to make ejaculatory prayer a substitute for public or family worship or for secret devotion; but it is a blessed resource, at our command under circumstances when other forms of prayer may be impossible. Toilers in the busy marts of trade, crowded and almost overwhelmed with financial perplexities; travelers by sea and land, when threatened by some great danger, can thus commit themselves to divine guidance and protection. And in every circumstance and condition of life, the soul weighed down with grief or care, or assailed by temptation, may thus find comfort, support, and succor in the unfailing love and power of a covenant-keeping God.

All things are possible to those who believe. No one who comes to the Lord in sincerity of heart will be disappointed. How wonderful it is that we can pray effectually; that unworthy, erring mortals possess the power of offering their requests to God! What higher power can man require than this,—to be linked-with the infinite God? Feeble, sinful man has the privilege of speaking to his Maker. We utter words that reach the throne of the Monarch of the universe. We pour out our heart's desire in our closets. Then we go forth to walk with God as did Enoch and Nehemiah.

We speak with Christ as we walk by the way, and he says, "I am at thy right hand." We may walk in daily companionship with him. When we breathe out our desire, it may be inaudible to any human ear; but that word can not die away in silence, nor can it be lost, though the activities of business are going on. Nothing can drown the soul's desire. Above the din of the street, above the noise of machinery, it rises to the heavenly courts. It is God to whom we are speaking, and the prayer is heard. Ask then; "ask, and it shall be given you."

Nehemiah and Artaxerxes stood face to face,—the one a servant, of a downtrodden race, the other the monarch of the world's great empire. But infinitely greater than the disparity of rank was the moral distance which separated them. Nehemiah had complied with the invitation of the King of kings, "Let him take hold of my strength, that he may make peace with me, and he shall make peace with me." The silent petition that he sent up to Heaven was the same that he had offered for many weeks, that God would prosper his request. And now, taking courage at the thought that he had a Friend, omniscient and omnipotent, to work in his behalf, the man of God made known to the king his desire for release for a time from his office at the court, and for authority to build up the waste places of Jerusalem and make it once more a strong and defensed city. Momentous results to the Jewish city and nation hung upon this request. And, says Nehemiah, "the king granted me according to the good hand of my God upon me."

—Southern Watchman, March 8, 1904

Chapter 3

Prudence and Forethought

While Nehemiah implored the help of God, he did not fold his own hands, feeling that he had no more care or responsibility in the bringing about of his purpose to restore Jerusalem. With admirable prudence and forethought he proceeded to make all the arrangements necessary to insure the success of the enterprise. Every movement was marked with great caution. He did not reveal his purpose even to his own countrymen; for while they would rejoice in his success, he feared that, by some indiscretion, they might hinder his work. Some would be liable to manifest exultation that would arouse the jealousy of their enemies, and perhaps cause the defeat of the undertaking.

As his request to the king had been so favorably received, he was encouraged to ask for such assistance as was needed for the carrying out of his plans. To give dignity and authority to his mission, as well as to provide for protection on the journey, he secured a military escort. He obtained royal letters to the governors of the provinces beyond the Euphrates, the territory through which he must pass on his way to Judea; and he obtained, also, a letter to the keeper of the king's forest in the mountains of Lebanon, directing him to furnish such timber as would be needed for the wall of Jerusalem and the buildings that Nehemiah proposed to erect. In order that there might be no occasion for complaint that he had exceeded his commission, Nehemiah was careful to have the authority and privileges accorded him, clearly defined.

The example of this holy man should be a lesson to all the people of God, that they are not only to pray in faith, but to work with diligence and fidelity. How many difficulties we encounter, how often we hinder the working of Providence in our behalf, because prudence, forethought, and painstaking are regarded as having little to do with religion! This is a grave mistake. It is our duty to cultivate and to exercise every power that will render us more efficient workers for God. Careful consideration and well-matured plans are as essential to the success of sacred enterprises today as in the time of Nehemiah. If all who are engaged in the Lord's work would realize how much depends upon their fidelity and wise forethought, far greater prosperity would attend their efforts. Through diffidence and backwardness we often fail of securing that which is attainable as a right, from the powers that be. God will work for us, when we are ready to do what we can and should do on our part.

Men of prayer should be men of action. Those who are ready and willing, will find ways and means of working. Nehemiah did not depend upon uncertainties. The means which he lacked he solicited from those who were able to bestow.

The Lord still moves upon the hearts of kings and rulers in behalf of his people. Those who are laboring for him are to avail themselves of the help that he prompts men to give for the advancement of his cause. The agents through whom these gifts come, may open ways by which the light of truth shall be given to many benighted lands. These men may have no sympathy with God's work, no faith in Christ, no acquaintance with his word; but their gifts are not on this account to be refused.

The Lord has placed his goods in the hands of unbelievers as well as believers; all may return to him his own for the doing of the work that must be done for a fallen world. As long as we are in this world, as long as the Spirit of God strives with the children of men, so long are we to receive favors as well as to impart them. We are to give to the world the light of truth, as revealed in the Scriptures; and we are to receive from the world that which God moves upon them to give in behalf of his cause.

The Lord's work might receive far greater favors than it is now receiving, if we would approach men in wisdom, acquainting them with the work, and giving them an opportunity of doing that which it is our privilege to induce them to do for its advancement. If we, as God's servants, would take a wise and prudent course his good hand would prosper us in our efforts.

Some may question the propriety of receiving gifts from unbelievers. Let such ask themselves: "Who is the real owner of our world? To whom belong its houses and lands, and its treasures of gold and silver?" God has an abundance in our world, and he has placed his goods in the hands of all, both the obedient and the disobedient. He is ready to move upon the hearts of worldly men, even idolaters, to give of their abundance for the support of his work; and he will do this as soon as his people learn to approach these men wisely and to call their attention to that which it is their privilege to do. If the needs of the Lord's work were set forth in a proper light before those who have means and influence, these men might do much to advance the cause of present truth. God's people have lost many privileges of which they could have taken advantage, had they not chosen to stand independent of the world.

In the providence of God, we are daily brought into connection hand God is preparing the way before us, in order that his work may progress rapidly. As co-laborers with him, we have a sacred, solemn work to do. We are to have travail of soul for those who are in high places: we are to extend to them the gracious invitation to come to the marriage feast.

Although now almost wholly in the possession of wicked men, all the world, with its riches and treasures, belongs to God. "The earth is the Lord's, and the fulness thereof." "The silver is mine, and the gold is mine, saith the Lord of hosts." "Every beast of the forest is mine, and the cattle upon a thousand hills. I know all the birds of the mountains; and the wild beasts of the field are mine. If I were hungry, I would not tell thee; for the world is mine, and the fulness thereof." O that Christians might realize more and still more fully that it is their privilege and their duty, while cherishing right principles, to take advantage of every heaven-sent opportunity for advancing God's kingdom in this world!

—Southern Watchman, March 15, 1904

Chapter 4

A Night of Preparation

The royal letters to the governors of the provinces along his route, secured to Nehemiah an honorable reception and prompt assistance. And no enemy dared molest the official who was guarded by the power of the Persian king and treated with marked consideration by the provincial rulers. Nehemiah's journey was safe and prosperous.

His arrival at Jerusalem, however, with the attendance of a military guard, showing that he had come on some important mission, excited the jealousy and hatred of the enemies of Israel. The heathen tribes settled near Jerusalem had previously indulged their enmity against the Jews by heaping upon them every insult and injury which they dared inflict. Foremost in this evil work were certain chiefs of these tribes, Sanballat the Horonite, Tobiah the Ammonite, and Geshem the Arabian; and from this time these leaders watched with jealous eye the movements of Nehemiah, and endeavored by every means in their power to thwart his plans and hinder his work.

Nehemiah continued to exercise the same caution and prudence that had hitherto marked his course. Knowing that bitter and determined enemies stood ready to oppose every effort for the restoration of Jerusalem, he concealed the nature of his mission until a study of the situation had enabled him to form his plans. Thus he was prepared to secure the cooperation of the people, and set them at work before his enemies had opportunity to arouse their fears or their prejudice.

Nehemiah had been highly honored of God, and had been entrusted with great responsibilities; but he did not, because of this, presume to act in an independent, self-sufficient manner. He selected a few persons whom he knew to be worthy of confidence, and to them he make known the circumstances that had led to his visit to Jerusalem, the object to be accomplished, and the plans that he purposed to employ. Thus he secured their assistance in his important undertaking.

On the third night after his arrival, the burden weighing so heavily upon his mind as to prevent sleep, he rose at midnight, and with a few trusted companions went out to view for himself the desolation of Jerusalem. Mounted on his mule, he moved about by moonlight, surveying the ruined walls and broken gates of the city of his fathers. Painful were the reflections that filled the mind of the Jewish patriot. Memories of Israel's past glory stood out in sharp contrast with the evidences of her present degradation. Because she had disregarded the word of God, rejected reproof, and refused to correct her ways, she had been left to be thus reduced in power and honor among the nations. The people for whom God had so wonderfully wrought, had trifled with their privileges, set at naught his counsels, and joined themselves to his enemies, until he had withdrawn from them his special presence and protection.

With sorrow-stricken heart, the visitor from afar gazed upon the ruined defenses of his loved Jerusalem. And is it not thus that angels of heaven survey the condition of the church of Christ? Like the dwellers at Jerusalem, we become accustomed to existing evils, and often are content while making no effort to remedy them. But how are these evils regarded by beings divinely illuminated? Do not they, like Nehemiah, look with sorrow-burdened heart upon ruined walls, and gates burned with fire?

Are not everywhere visible the shameful tokens of backsliding from God and conformity with a sin-loving and truth-hating word? In these days of darkness and peril, who is able to stand in defense of Zion and show her any good? Her spiritual state and prospects are not in accordance with the light and privileges bestowed of God.

To many of the professed followers of Christ today are applicable the same reproofs that were given to the people of Israel when the Lord said by his prophets, "Thus have they loved to wander, they have not refrained their feet, therefore the Lord doth not accept them; he will now remember their iniquity and visit their sins."

In secrecy and silence, Nehemiah completed his circuit of the walls. He declares, "The rulers knew not whither I went, or what I did; neither had I as yet told it to the Jews , nor to the priests, nor to the nobles, nor to the rulers, nor to the rest that did the work." In this painful survey he did not wish to attract the attention of either friends or foes, lest an excitement should be created, and reports be put in circulation that might defeat, or at least hinder, his work.

Nehemiah devoted the remainder of the night to prayer; in the morning there must be earnest effort to arouse and unite his dispirited and divided countrymen.

—Southern Watchman, March 22, 1904

Chapter 5

Securing The Cooperation Of The People

Although Nehemiah bore a royal commission requiring the inhabitants to cooperate with him in rebuilding the walls of the city, he chose not to depend upon the mere exercise of authority. He sought rather to gain the confidence and sympathy of the people, well knowing that a union of hearts as well as hands was essential to success in the great work which he had undertaken. When he called the people together on the morrow, he presented such arguments as were calculated to arouse their dormant energies and to unite their scattered numbers.

They knew not, neither did he tell them, of his mournful midnight circuit while they were sleeping. Nevertheless that very circumstance contributed greatly to his success. He was enabled to speak of the condition of the city with an accuracy and minuteness that astonished his hearers, while the actual contemplation of the weakness and degradation of Israel, deeply impressing his heart, gave earnestness and power to his words. He presented before the people their condition as objects of reproach among the heathen. The nation once so highly favored of God as to excite the terror of all surrounding countries, had now become a byword and a hissing. Her religion was dishonored, her God blasphemed.

He then told them how, in a distant land, he had heard of their affliction, how he had entreated the favor of God in their behalf, and how, while praying, the plan had been formed in his mind, of soliciting permission from the king to come to their assistance. He had asked God that the king might not only allow him to go to Jerusalem, but invest him with authority and render the help needed for the work. His prayer had been answered in such a manner as clearly to show that the whole thing was of the Lord. And having laid the matter fully before them, showing that he was sustained by the combined authority of the Persian king and the God of Israel, Nehemiah put to the people directly the question whether they would take advantage of this favorable occasion, and arise with him and build the wall.

This appeal went straight to their hearts; the manifestation of the favor of heaven toward them put their fears to shame. With new courage they cried out with one voice, "Let us rise up and build."

The holy energy and high hope of Nehemiah were communicated to the people. As they caught the spirit,they rose for a time to the moral level of their leader. Each, in his own sphere, was a sort of Nehemiah; and each strengthened and upheld his brother in the work.

There is need of Nehemiahs in the church today,— not men who can pray and preach only, but men whose prayers and sermons are braced with firm and eager purpose. The course pursued by this Hebrew patriot in the accomplishment of his plans is one that should still be adopted by ministers and leading men. When they have laid their plans, they should present them to the church in such a manner as to win their interest and cooperation. Let the people understand the plans and share in the work, and they will have a personal interest in its prosperity. The success attending Nehemiah's efforts shows what prayer, faith, and wise, energetic action will accomplish. Living faith will prompt to energetic action. The spirit manifested by the leader will be, to a great extent, reflected by the people. If the leaders professing to believe the solemn, important truths that are to test the world at this time, manifest no ardent zeal to prepare a people to stand in the day of God, we must expect the church to be careless, indolent, and pleasure-loving.

—*Southern Watchman, March 29, 1904*

Chapter 6

"Zealous of Good Works"

Among the first to catch Nehemiah's spirit of zeal and earnestness were the priests of Israel. From the position of influence which they occupied, these men could do much to hinder or advance the work. Their ready cooperation at the very outset contributed not a little to its success. Thus should it be in every holy enterprise. Those who occupy positions of influence and responsibility in the church, should be foremost in the work of

God. If they move reluctantly, others will not move at all. But "their zeal will provoke very many." When their light burns brightly, a thousand torches will be kindled at the flame.

A majority of the nobles and rulers of Israel also came nobly up to their duty; but there were a few, the Tekoite nobles, who "put not their necks to the work of their Lord." While the faithful builders have honorable mention in the book of God, the memory of these slothful servants is branded with shame, and handed down as a warning to all future generations.

In every religious movement there are some who, while they can not deny that it is the work of God, will keep themselves aloof, refusing to make any effort to advance it. But in enterprises to promote their selfish interests, these men are often the most active and energetic workers. It were well to remember that record kept on high, the book of God, in which all our motives and our works are written—that book in which there are no omissions, no mistakes, and out of which we are to be judged. There every neglected opportunity to do service for God will be faithfully reported, and every deed of faith and love, however humble, will be held in everlasting remembrance. Against the inspiring influence of Nehemiah's presence, the example of the Tekoite nobles had little weight. The people in general were animated with one heart and one soul of patriotism and cheerful activity. Men of ability and influence organized the various classes of citizens into companies, each leader making himself responsible for the erection of a certain portion of the wall. It was a sight well pleasing to God and angels to see the busy companies, working harmoniously upon the broken-down walls of Jerusalem, and it was a joyous sound to hear, the noise of instruments of labor from the earliest dawn "till the stars appeared."

Nehemiah's zeal and energy did not abate, now that the work was actually begun. He did not fold his hands, feeling that he might let fall the burden. With tireless vigilance he constantly superintended the work, directing the workmen, noting every hindrance, and providing for every emergency. His influence was constantly felt along the whole extent of those three miles of wall. With timely words he encouraged the fearful, approved the diligent, or aroused the laggard. And again he watched with eagle eye the movements of their enemies, who at times collected at a distance and engaged in earnest conversation, as if plotting mischief, and then drawing near the workmen attempted to divert their attention and hinder the work. While the eye of every worker is often directed to Nehemiah, ready to heed the slightest signal, his eye and heart are uplifted to God, the great Overseer of the whole work, the One who put it into the heart of his servant to build. And as faith and courage strengthen in his own heart, Nehemiah exclaims, and his words, repeated and re-echoed, thrill the hearts of the workers all along the line, "The God of heaven, he will prosper us!"

—*Southern Watchman, April 5, 1904*

Chapter 7

Derision And Discouragement

Those who were restoring the defenses of Jerusalem did not go forward in their work unmolested. Satan was busy in stirring up opposition and creating discouragement. The principal agents in this movement were Sanballat the Horonite, Tobiah the Ammonite, and Geshem the Arabian. These idolaters had exulted in the feeble and defenseless condition of the Jews, and had mocked at their religion, and ridiculed their devastated city. And when the work of rebuilding the wall was entered upon, they, with envenomed zeal, set themselves to hinder the undertaking, To accomplish this, they attempted to cause division among the workmen by suggesting doubts and arousing unbelief as to their success. They also ridiculed the efforts of the builders, declared the enterprise an impossibility, and predicted a disgraceful failure.

"What do these feeble Jews?" exclaimed Sanballat, mockingly. "Will they fortify themselves? will they sacrifice? will they make an end in a day? will they revive the stones out of the heaps of the rubbish which are burned?" Tobiah, endeavoring to be still more contemptuous and sarcastic, added, "Even that which they build, if a fox go up, he shall even break down their stone wall."

The builders on the wall were soon beset by more active opposition. They were compelled to guard continually against the plots of their sleepless adversaries. The emissaries of the enemy endeavored to destroy their courage by the circulation of false reports; conspiracies were formed on various pretexts to draw Nehemiah into their toils; and falsehearted Jews were found ready to aid the treacherous undertaking. Again, the report was spread that Nehemiah was plotting rebellion against the Persian monarch, intending to exalt himself as king over Israel, and that all who aided him were traitors.

Emissaries of the enemy, professing friendliness, mingled with the builders, suggesting changes in the plan, seeking in various ways to divert the attention of the workers, to cause confusion and perplexity, and to arouse distrust and suspicion. And the plans formed for the advancement of the work were reported, by these spies, to the enemy, and thus they were enabled to labor with greater effect to thwart the purpose of the builders.

But Nehemiah continued to look to God for guidance and support, and the work went forward until the gaps were filled, and the entire wall built up to half its intended height. As the enemies of Israel saw that all their efforts had been unavailing, they were filled with rage. Hitherto they had not dared to employ violent measures; for Nehemiah and his companions were acting by the king's commission, and any active opposition might bring upon themselves the monarch's displeasure. But now, in their blind passion, they themselves became guilty of the crime of rebellion of which they had so eagerly accused Nehemiah. Having assembled for united counsel, they "conspired all of them together to come and to fight against Jerusalem."

The experience of Nehemiah is repeated in the history of God's people in this time. Those who labor in the cause of truth will find that they can not do this without exciting the anger of its enemies. Though they have been called of God to the work in which they are engaged, and their course is approved of him, they can not escape reproach and derision. They will be denounced as visionary, unreliable, scheming, hypocritical,—anything, in short, that will suit the purpose of their enemies. The most sacred things will be represented in a ridiculous light to amuse the ungodly. A very small amount of sarcasm and low wit, united with envy, jealousy, impiety, and hatred, is sufficient to excite the mirth of the profane scoffer. And these presumptuous jesters sharpen one another's ingenuity, and embolden each other in their blasphemous work. Contempt and derision are indeed painful to human nature; but they must be endured by all who are true to God. It is the policy of Satan thus to turn souls from doing the work which the Lord has laid upon them.

Proud scorners are not to be trusted; yet, as Satan found in the heavenly courts a company to sympathize with him, so these find among professed followers of Christ those whom they can influence, who believe them honest, who sympathize with them, plead in their behalf, and become permeated with their spirit. Those who are at variance in almost everything else, will unite in persecuting the few who dare to pursue the straightforward path of duty. And the same enmity which leads to contempt and derision, will, at a favorable opportunity, inspire more violent and cruel measures, especially when workers for God are active and successful.

—*Southern Watchman, April 12, 1904*

Chapter 8

Disaffection Among the Unbelieving

Some of the leading men among the Jews, becoming disaffected, sought to discourage Nehemiah by exaggerating the difficulties attending the work, and they represented the people as already exhausted by their excessive labor. Said they, "The strength of the bearers of burdens is decayed, and there is much rubbish; so that we are not able to build the wall."

Again, they attempted to intimidate the people by the report that large armies were preparing for a secret attack upon the city: "And our adversaries said, They shall not know, neither see, till we come in the midst among them, and slay them, and cause the work to cease." It was the help and encouragement received from traitors in the camp that emboldened the enemies of Israel to make those threats. And traitors reported the threats for the sole purpose of terrifying and disheartening the builders on the wall.

"And it came to pass, that when the Jews which dwelt by them came, they said unto us ten times, From all places whence ye shall return unto us they will be upon you." These alarms were given by those who were taking no part in the work. They were gathering up the statements and reports of their enemies, and bringing these in to the workers to weaken courage and create disaffection. Then every word of complaint, distrust, suspicion, or unbelief dropped by the workmen, with all the additional conjectures and conclusions of the news-carriers, was eagerly reported outside the walls, and circulated among those who despised the Jews, and sought to hinder their prosperity.

The same difficulties are experienced by those who are now seeking to make up the breach in the law of God. The servants of the Lord must expect every kind of discouragement. They will be tried, not only by the anger, contempt, and cruelty of enemies, but by the indolence, inconsistency, lukewarmness, and treachery

31

of friends and helpers. As we seek to advance the cause of truth, and prepare a people to stand in the day of God, we are led directly away from the customs and practices of the world. But there are among us pleasure-seekers, who are not laboring to meet the high standard of the divine requirements, who love the spirit and influence of the world more than they love the truth or the prosperity of God's cause. These unconsecrated elements are used by Satan to accomplish his purposes. While still connected with the people of God, they unite themselves with his enemies, and thus the Lord's work is laid open to the attacks of its bitterest foes, and the arguments furnished by professed friends of the truth are employed to destroy the confidence, courage, and faith of workers who are too easily discouraged.

Even some who seem to desire the work of God to prosper, will yet weaken the hands of his servants by hearing, reporting, and half believing the slanders, boasts, and menaces of their adversaries. Those who appear to be honest souls are sometimes deceived through the influence of ambitious and turbulent men. Satan works with marvelous success through his agents; and all who yield to their influence are subject to a bewitching power that destroys the wisdom of the wise and the understanding of the prudent. Hence they allow themselves to be prejudiced, misled, and deceived. For this reason, many whose lives are a reproach to the cause of truth, will yet succeed in arousing distrust and suspicion of those through whom God is working.

How busy, in a crisis, is the rebellious spirit, the evil tongue! How eagerly will they gather up floating rumors, and send them to the bitterest enemies of God, to be sown broadcast, like thistle-seed, to produce their harvest of evil! And when the result is seen, in desolation, backsliding, and apostasy, then those who have done the very work which Satan prompted them to do, are ready to charge the result upon the faithful workers whom they have hindered, burdened, and distressed. But every man's work stands registered in the books of heaven, and no disguise can there conceal the motives that prompt to action. Those who obey God will be honored of him.

Amid great discouragements, Nehemiah made God his trust; and here is our defense. A remembrance of what the Lord has done for us will prove a support in every danger. "He that spared not his own Son, but delivered him up for us all, how shall he not with him also freely give us all things?" And "if God be for us, who can be against us?" However craftily the plots of Satan and his agents may be laid, God can detect them, and bring to naught all their counsels.

—*Southern Watchman, April 19, 1904*

Chapter 9

Courageous Perseverance

The most bitter opposition, the boldest threats of the enemy, seemed only to inspire Nehemiah with firmer determination, and to arouse him to greater watchfulness. "Nevertheless," he declares, "we made our prayer unto our God, and set a watch against them day and night." "Therefore set I in the lower places behind the wall, and on the higher places, I even set the people after their families with their swords, their spears, and their bows. And I looked, and rose up, and said unto the nobles, and to the rulers, and to the rest of the people, Be not ye afraid of them; remember the Lord, which is great and terrible, and fight for your brethren, your sons, and your daughters, your wives, and your houses. And it came to pass, when our enemies heard that it was known unto us, and God had brought their counsel to naught, that we returned all of us to the wall, every one unto his work. And it came to pass from that time forth, that the half of my servants wrought in the work, and the other half of them held both the spears, the shields, and the bows, and the habergeons." "They which builded on the wall, and they that bare burdens, with those that laded, every one with one of his hands wrought in the work, and with the other hand held a weapon. For the builders, every one had his sword girded by his side, and so builded."

Beside Nehemiah stood a trumpeter, and on different parts of the wall were stationed priests bearing the sacred trumpets. The people were scattered in their labors; but on the approach of danger at any point, a signal was given for them to repair thither without delay. Then the priests sounded an alarm upon the trumpets as a token that God would fight for them. "So we labored in the work," says Nehemiah; "and half of them held the spears from the rising of the morning till the stars appeared." Those who lived in towns and villages outside Jerusalem were required to lodge within the walls, both to guard the work and that they might be ready for duty in the morning. This would prevent unnecessary delay, and, furthermore, would cut off the opportunity, which the enemies would otherwise enjoy, of attacking the workmen as they went to and from their homes, or embittering with prejudice or discouraging by threats.

Nehemiah and his companions did not shrink from hardships, or excuse themselves from trying service. Neither by night nor by day, not even during the brief time given to slumber, did they put off their clothing, or even lay aside their armor. "So neither I, nor my brethren, nor my servants, nor the men of the guard which followed me, none of us put off our clothes, saving that every one put them off for washing."

Nehemiah was engaged in an important work, one which concerned the prosperity of the cause of God. Every effort previously put forth to accomplish that work had failed because of a lack of true faith and union of effort among the Jews. The Samaritans, disguising their enmity under a pretense of fidelity to the king of Persia, had succeeded in causing a discontinuance of the work. The zealous and truehearted among the Jews had again and again been disappointed in their purposes. But in the strength of God, Nehemiah determined that the adversaries should not again hinder the work. The despisers of the God of heaven should be disappointed. Their Satanic policy could not succeed if the people of God would bar the doors against the enemy, and work harmoniously to carry out the divine will. The foe could not enter unless the gates were thrown open by traitors within.

If we are but loyal and true, every attack of the enemy will lead us to a firmer reliance upon God, and to more determined effort to carry forward his work, against all opposing influences.

"Know therefore that the Lord thy God, he is God, the faithful God, which keepeth covenant and mercy with them that love him and keep his commandments to a thousand generations."

—Southern Watchman, April 26, 1904

Chapter 10

A Rebuke Against Extortioners

The wall of Jerusalem had not been completed, when Nehemiah's attention was called to the unhappy condition of the poorer classes of the people. In the unsettled state of the country, tillage had been, to some extent, neglected. Furthermore, because of their separation from God his blessing had not rested upon their lands. A scarcity of grain resulted. To obtain food for their families, the poor were obliged to buy on credit, and at an exorbitant price. They were also compelled to raise money by borrowing on interest, to pay the tribute to the king of Persia. The people of Israel were not now enjoying prosperity, as when the Lord blessed them for their obedience. Because of their sins, their defense had been removed, and the Lord had allowed other nations to overcome them. Under the rule of idolatrous kings, heavy taxes were imposed upon them; property, liberty, and life seemed at the mercy of these godless powers.

While they had no thought of revolting against the king of Persia, they had hoped, by repentance and reformation, to regain the favor of God, and to be restored to their former liberty. As yet their hopes were not realized. The tribute money for the king must be forthcoming in its season. To add to the distress of the poor, the more wealthy took advantage of their necessity, obtaining mortgages of their lands, and adding them to their own large possessions. They also required usury for all money loaned. This course soon reduced the unfortunate debtors to the deepest poverty, and many were forced to sell their sons and daughters to servitude. There appeared no hope of improving their condition, no way to regain either their lands or their children, no prospect before them but that of perpetual slavery. And yet they were of the same nation, children of the covenant equally with their more favored brethren. They had the same affection for their children as had the others. Their distress had not been caused by indolence or prodigality. They had been compelled to contract debts because of the failure of crops, and to pay heavy taxes.

As a last resort, they presented their case before Nehemiah. The soul of this man of God was filled with indignation as he heard of the cruel oppression that existed among his own people. He resolved to see that justice was done; yet he did not move rashly in the matter. He felt that God had laid upon him grave responsibilities, and he must be faithful to his trust. "I was very angry," he says, "when I heard their cry and these words. Then I consulted with myself." He took time to weigh the whole matter, and to form plans. Then with characteristic energy and determination, he exerted his influence and authority for the relief of his oppressed brethren.

The fact that the oppressors were men of wealth, whose support was greatly needed in the work of restoring the city and its defenses, did not for a moment turn him from his purpose. Having first sharply rebuked the nobles and rulers, he presented the matter in an assembly of the people, clearly showing what were the requirements of God touching the case, and urging them upon the attention of his hearers.

Similar events had occurred in the reign of the apostate Ahaz, and God sent a message to Israel, rebuking their cruelty and oppression. The children of Judah, because of their idolatry, had been delivered into the hands of their more idolatrous brethren, the people of Israel. The latter had indulged their cruel enmity by slaying in battle many thousands of the men of Judah, and seizing all the women and children, intending to keep them as slaves, or sell them into bondage to the heathen.

Because of the sins of Judah, the Lord had not interposed to prevent the battle; but by the mouth of the prophet Oded he rebuked the cruel design of the victorious army: "Ye purpose to keep under the children of Judah and Jerusalem for bondmen and bondwomen unto you; but are there not with you, even with you, sins against the Lord your God?" And the prophet assured them that the fierce anger of the Lord was upon them, and that their course of injustice and oppression would call down his judgments. Upon hearing these words, the armed men left the captives and the spoil before the princes and all the congregation. Then certain leading men of the tribe of Ephraim "took the captives, and with the spoil clothed all that were naked among them, and arrayed them, and shod them, and gave them to eat and to drink, and anointed them, and carried all the feeble of them upon asses, and brought them to Jericho, the city of palm-trees, to their brethren."

Nehemiah wished to bring the offenders to see the real character of their oppressive work, and to be ashamed of it. Said he, "We, after our ability, have redeemed our brethren the Jews, which were sold unto the heathen; and will ye even sell your brethren? or shall they be sold unto us?" Nehemiah and others had ransomed certain of the Jews who had been sold to the heathen, and he now placed this course in contrast with the conduct of those who for worldly gain were enslaving their brethren. The fear of God should restrain them from such injustice. Nehemiah declared to the Jewish rulers—some of whom had been guilty of these practices—that instead of judging and punishing other criminals, they should investigate their own work, and cease at once their iniquitous extortion, lest they should become a reproach, even among the heathen.

He showed them that he himself, being invested with authority from the Persian king, might have demanded large contributions for his personal benefit. Instead of this, he had not taken that which justly belonged to him, but had liberally contributed to relieve the people in their great necessity. These extortioners had no more reason than he had to pursue the course they did. He urged them to cease at once their oppression, to restore the lands of the poor, and also the increase of money and provisions which they had exacted from them, and to lend them without security or usury.

"Then said they, We will restore them, and will require nothing of them; so will we do as thou sayest." "Then," says Nehemiah, "I called the priests, and took an oath of them, that they should do according to this promise."

—*Southern Watchman, May 3, 1904*

Chapter 11

Integrity in Business Affairs

These portions of sacred history teach an important lesson. Those who profess to love and fear God should cherish sympathy and love for one another, and should guard the interests of others as their own. Christians should not regulate their conduct by the world's standard. In all ages the people of God are as distinct from worldlings as their profession is higher than that of the ungodly. From the beginning to the end of time, God's people are one body.

The love of money is the root of all evil. In this generation the desire for gain is the absorbing passion. If wealth can not be secured by honest industry, men seek to obtain it by fraud. Widows and orphans are robbed of their scanty pittance, and poor men are made to suffer for the necessaries of life. And all this that the rich may support their extravagance, or indulge their desire to hoard.

The terrible record of crime daily committed for the sake of gain, is enough to chill the blood and fill the soul with horror. The fact that even among those who profess godliness the same sins exist to a greater or less extent, calls for deep humiliation of soul and earnest action on the part of the followers of Christ. Love of display and love of money have made this world a den of thieves and robbers. But Christians are professedly not dwellers upon the earth; they are in a strange country, stopping, as it were, only for a night. They should not be actuated by the same motives and desires as are those who have their home and treasure here. God designed that our lives should represent the life of our great Pattern: that, like Jesus, we should live to do others good.

The customs of the world are no criterion for the Christian. He is not to imitate their sharp practice, over-reaching, and extortion, even in a small matters. Every unjust act toward a fellow-mortal,though he be the veriest sinner, is a violation of the golden rule. Every wrong done to the children of God, is done to Christ himself in the person of his saints. Every attempt to advantage one's self by the ignorance, weakness, or misfortune of another, is registered as fraud in the ledger of heaven.

He who truly fears God would rather toil day and night, and eat the bread of poverty, than to indulge a passion for gain which would oppress the widow and the fatherless, or turn the stranger from his right. Our Saviour sought to impress upon his hearers that a man who would venture to defraud his neighbor in the smallest item, would, if the opportunity were favorable, overreach in larger matters. The slightest departure from rectitude breaks down the barriers, and prepares the heart to do greater injustice. By precept and example, Christ taught that the strictest integrity should govern our conduct toward our fellow-men. Said the divine Teacher, "Whatsoever ye would that men should do to you, do ye even so to them."

Just to the extent that man would advantage himself at the disadvantage of another, will his soul become insensible to the influence of the Spirit of God. Gain obtained at such a cost is a fearful loss. It is better to want than to lie; better to hunger than to defraud; better to die than to sin. Extravagance, overreaching, extortion indulged by those professing godliness, are corrupting their faith, and destroying their spirituality. The church is in a great degree responsible for the sins of her members. She gives countenance to the evil, if she fails to lift her voice against it. The influence from which she has most to fear is not that of open opposers, infidels, and blasphemers, but of inconsistent professors of Christ. These are the ones who keep back the blessing of the God of Israel.

All who would form characters for heaven must be Bible Christians. They must be diligent in the study of the Chart of Life, and must carefully and prayerfully examine the motives that prompt them to action. The business world does not lie outside the limits of God's government. True religion is not to be merely paraded on the Sabbath, and displayed in the sanctuary; it is for every day and for every place. Its claims must be recognized and obeyed in every act of life. Men who possess the genuine article will in all their business affairs show as clear a perception of right, as when offering their supplications at the throne of grace.

God can not be excluded from any transaction in which the rights of his children are concerned. Over every one that is serving him in sincerity, his hand is spread as a buckler. None can wound the humblest disciple of Jesus without smiting that hand which holds the sword of justice.

The apostle James, looking down to the last days, addresses a solemn and fearful warning to those who have heaped up riches by fraud and oppression: "Go to now, ye rich men, weep and howl for your miseries that shall come upon you. Your riches are corrupted, and your garments are moth-eaten. Your gold and silver is cankered; and the rust of them shall be a witness against you, and shall eat your flesh as it were fire. Ye have heaped treasure together for the last days. Behold, the hire of the laborers who have reaped down your fields, which is of you kept back by fraud, crieth; and the cries of them which have reaped are entered into the ears of the Lord of sabaoth."

—*Southern Watchman, May 10, 1904*

Chapter 12

Heathen Plots—No. 1

Sanballat, Tobiah, and their confederates dared not openly make war upon the Jews; but with increasing malice they continued their secret efforts to perplex, injure, and discourage them. The wall about Jerusalem was rapidly approaching completion. When it should be finished, and its gates set up, these enemies of Israel could not hope to force an entrance into the city. Therefore they were the more eager and determined in their efforts to stop the work without delay. At last they devised a plan to draw Nehemiah from his station, and kill or imprison him while they had him in their power.

Pretending to desire a compromise of the opposing parties, they proposed a conference with Nehemiah, and invited him to meet them in a village on the plain of Ono. But the Spirit of God, enlightening the mind of his servant, enabled him to discern their real purpose. Nehemiah says, "I sent messengers unto them, saying, I am doing a great work, so that I can not come down; why should the work cease, whilst I leave it and come down to you?" But these emissaries of Satan were persistent. Four times they sent messages of like import, but received the same answer.

Finding this plan unsuccessful, they then had resort to a more dangerous stratagem. Sanballat sent to Nehemiah a messenger bearing an open letter wherein was written: "It is reported among the heathen, and Gashmu saith it, that thou and the Jews think to rebel; for which cause thou buildest the wall, that thou mayest be their king, according to these words. And thou hast also appointed prophets to preach of thee at Jerusalem, saying, There is a king in Judah; and now shall it be reported to the king according to these words. Come now therefore, and let us take counsel together."

Had the reports mentioned been actually circulated, there would have been cause for apprehension; for they would soon have been carried to the ears of the king, whom a slight suspicion might provoke to the severest measures. But Nehemiah was convinced that the letter was wholly false, written to arouse his fears, and draw him into some snare prepared by his enemies. This conclusion was strengthened by the fact that the letter was sent open, evidently that the contents might be read by the people, and thus intimidate them also.

He therefore promptly returned the answer, "There are no such things done as thou sayest, but thou feignest them out of thine own heart." He is not ignorant of Satan's devices, and he feels assured that all these attempts are made for the purpose of weakening the hands of the builders, that their work may not be accomplished. He turns to the Source of strength, with the prayer, "Now therefore, O God, strengthen my hands."

Satan had been defeated again and again; and now with deeper malice and greater cunning, he proceeded to devise a still more subtle and dangerous snare for the servant of God. Sanballat and his companions were moved to hire men professing to be friends of Nehemiah, to give him evil counsel as the word of the Lord. The principal person engaged in this nefarious work was one Shemaiah, who had previously been held in good repute by Nehemiah. This man shut himself up in a chamber near the sanctuary, as if fearing that his life was in danger, and thither Nehemiah went to consult with him as one who was especially favored of God. The temple was at this time protected by walls and gates, while the gates of the city were not yet set up. This deceiver therefore professed great concern for Nehemiah's safety, and counseled him to seek shelter in the temple: "Let us meet together in the house of God, within the temple, and let us shut the doors of the temple; for they will come to slay thee; yea, in the night will they come to slay thee." The hero's fearless answer was, "Should such a man as I flee?

and who is there, that, being as I am, would go into the temple to save his life? I will not go in."

Had Nehemiah followed that treacherous counsel, he would have sacrificed his reputation for courage and faith in God, and would have appeared cowardly and contemptible. The alarm would have spread among the people: each would have sought his own safety; and the city would have been left unprotected, to fall a prey to their enemies. That one unwise move would have been a virtual surrender of all that had been gained.

Nehemiah was not long in penetrating the true character and object of his counselor: "And, lo, I perceived that God had not sent him: but that he pronounced this prophecy against me; for Tobiah and Sanballat had hired him. Therefore was he hired, that I should be afraid, and do so, and sin, and that they might have matter for an evil report, that they might reproach me."

In view of the important work that Nehemiah had undertaken, together with the integrity of his character, and the confidence in God which he professed to feel, it would be highly inconsistent for him to hide himself as if in fear. The preservation of life itself would not be a sufficient excuse for such a course. The infamous counsel given him was seconded by more than one man of high reputation, who, while professing to be his friend, was secretly in league with his enemies. Women also, while pretending to have received great light from God, basely sold themselves to serve the cause of the heathen. Nehemiah prays that God will mark their evil designs, and reward them according to their deeds.

—*Southern Watchman, May 17, 1904*

Chapter 13

Heathen Plots—No. 2

Despite all the plots of enemies, open and secret, the work of building went steadily forward, the wall rose to the proper height, and in about two months after Nehemiah's arrival at Jerusalem, the holy city was girded round with its defenses and the builders could walk upon its walls, and look forth upon their astonished adversaries. Says Nehemiah, "When all our enemies heard thereof, and all the heathen that were about us saw these things, they were much cast down in their own eyes; for they perceived that this work was wrought of our God."

Yet the striking evidence that the hand of the Lord was with Nehemiah was not sufficient to restrain discontent, rebellion, and treachery. "In those days the nobles of Judah sent many letters unto Tobiah, and the letters of Tobiah came unto them. For there were many in Judah sworn unto him because he was the son-in-law of Shechaniah. Here are seen the evil results of intermarriage with idolaters. In this union, Satan had gained the victory. A family of Judah had connected themselves with the enemies of God, and the relation had proved a snare to the people. Many others also united in marriage with the heathen. These, like the mixed multitude that came up with Israel from Egypt, were a source of constant trouble. They were not wholehearted in the service of God. When his work demanded a sacrifice, they were ready to violate their own solemn oaths of cooperation and support. All this had tended to weaken and discourage those who sought to build up the cause of God.

Some who had been foremost in plotting mischief against the Jews, and endeavoring by every possible means to cause their ruin, now professed a great desire to be on friendly terms with them. Some of the nobles of Judah who had become entangled in idolatrous marriages, had held traitorous correspondence with Tobiah, and had taken oath to serve him. They now presumed to represent this agent of Satan as a man of ability, wisdom, and foresight, and urged that an alliance with him would be highly advantageous to the Jews. At the same time they betrayed to him Nehemiah's plans and movements. Thus the work of God was laid open to his enemies, and opportunity was given them not only to misconstrue Nehemiah's words and acts, and circulate false reports concerning him, but to lay plans to counteract his efforts and hinder his work. Yet this man, who had so boldly stood in defense of the oppressed, did not exercise the authority with which he was invested, and bring to punishment these traitors in the camp. Calmly and unselfishly he went forward in the service of his people, never dreaming of slackening his efforts, though they should be repaid only with ingratitude and treachery.

The whole power and policy of Satan have always been aimed at those who are zealously seeking to advance the cause and work of God. Though often baffled, he as often renews his assaults. But it is when he works in secret that he is most to be feared. The advocates of unpopular truth must expect opposition from its open enemies; this is often fierce and cruel, but it is far less dangerous than the secret enmity of those who profess to be serving God while at heart they are servants of Satan. While apparently uniting in the work of God, many are connected with his foes; and if in any way crossed in their plans or reproved for their sins, they court the favor of the enemies of truth, and open to them all the plans of God's servants and the workings of his cause. Thus they place every advantage in the hands of those who use all their knowledge to hinder the work of God and injure his people. Thus these men of two minds and two purposes pretend to serve God, and then go over to the enemy and serve him, as best suits their inclination.

Every device which the prince of darkness can suggest, will be employed to induce God's servants to form a compromise with the agents of Satan. Repeated solicitations will come in to call us from duty; but, like Nehemiah, we should steadfastly reply, "I am doing a great work, so that I can not come down." We have no time to seek the favor of the world, or even to defend ourselves from their misrepresentation and calumny. We have no time to lose in self-vindication. We should keep steadily at our work, and let that refute the falsehoods which malice may coin to our injury. Slanders will be multiplied if we stop to answer them. Should we allow our enemies to gain our friendship and sympathy, and thereby allure us from our post of duty; should we, by any unguarded act, expose the cause of God to reproach, and thus weaken the hands of the workers, we should bring upon our characters a stain not easily removed, and place a serious obstacle in the way of our own future usefulness.

Those temptations are most dangerous which come from the professed servants of God, and from our friends. When persons who are uniting with the world, yet claiming great piety and love, counsel the faithful workers for God to be less zealous and more conservative, our answer must be an appeal to the word of God. When they plead for union with those who have been our determined opposers, we should fear and shun them as decidedly as did Nehemiah. Those who would lead away from the old landmarks to form a connection with the ungodly, can not be sent of heaven. Whatever may have been their former position, their present course tends to unsettle the faith of God's people.

Such counselors are prompted by Satan. They are timeservers. The testimonies, reproofs, and warnings of God's servants are unpalatable to them, being a reproof to their worldly, pleasure-loving propensities. We should shun this class as resolutely as did Nehemiah.

When plied with the arguments and suggestions of such advisers, it would be well for us each to inquire, "Should I, who am a Christian, a child of God; one called to be the light of the world, a preacher of righteousness; who have so often expressed my confidence in the truth and the way in which the Lord has led us,—should I unite my influence with those who bitterly oppose the work of God? Should I, a steward of the mysteries of God, open to his worst enemies the counsels of his people? Would not such a course embolden the wicked in their opposition to the truth of God and to his covenant-keeping people? Would not such concession prevent me from opening my lips in exhortation, warning, or entreaty in my own family or in the church of God? If Paul or Peter were placed in similar circumstances, would he thus betray a sacred trust? Would not even men of the world despise me? Would they not scorn to be diverted from their lifework by difficulties or perils?"

Satan will work by any and every means which he can employ to discourage the active servants of God. If the shepherd can be beguiled from his duty, then the way is clear for wolves to scatter and devour the sheep.

Every success of the truth discourages the enemies of God: and they are sometimes forced to acknowledge that it is his work, while they hate it the more on that very account. False brethren will continue to increase. Those to whom God has sent warnings and reproofs, but who, rejecting the heaven-sent message, give heed to the counsel of his enemies, are the severest trial to his faithful servants. "They that forsake the law, praise the wicked."

—Southern Watchman, May 24, 1904

Chapter 14

The People Instructed in the Law of God

While Nehemiah labored diligently to restore the material defenses of Jerusalem, he did not forget that the God of Israel was their only sure defense, and that only in obedience to his commandments would they be secure. He therefore gave diligent attention to the instruction of the people in the law of God.

At the time of the feast of trumpets, when many were gathered at the holy city, the people assembled in the street that was before the water gate; "and they spake unto Ezra the scribe to bring the book of the law of Moses, which the Lord had commanded to Israel. And Ezra the priest brought the law before the congregation both of men and women, and all that could hear with understanding, upon the first day of the seventh month. And he read therein before the street that was before the water gate from the morning until midday…. And the ears of all the people were attentive unto the book of the law."

"And Ezra blessed the Lord, the great God. And all the people answered Amen, Amen, with lifting up their hands; and they bowed their heads, and worshiped the Lord with their faces to the ground." Certain of the priests and Levites united with Ezra in explaining to the people the principles of the divine law. "So they read in the book in the law of God distinctly, and gave the sense, and caused them to understand the reading."

The scene was one of mournful interest. The wall of Jerusalem had been rebuilt, and the gates set up; thus far a great victory had been achieved; but a large part of the city was still in ruins. On a pulpit of wood, erected in one of the broadest streets, and surrounded on every hand by the sad reminders of Judah's departed glory, stood Ezra, now an aged man. At his right and left were gathered his brother Levites, who were consecrated to the service of God, and whose presence lent dignity and solemnity to the occasion. With heavy hearts they thought upon the days of their fathers, when the royal psalmist had sung: "Walk about Zion, and go round about her; tell the towers thereof. Mark ye well her bulwarks, consider her palaces." "Beautiful for situation, the joy of the whole earth, is Mount Zion, on the sides of the north, the city of the great King."

Looking down from the elevated platform, the eye swept over a sea of heads. From all the surrounding country the children of the covenant had assembled; and as one man they were listening, intent and reverent, to hear once more the words of the Most High.

But even here the evidence of their sin was apparent. In their mingling with other nations, the Hebrew language had become corrupted, and therefore great care was necessary on the part of the speakers to explain the law in the language of the people, and so present it that it might be understood by all.

As the law of God was read and explained, the people were convinced of their guilt and danger, and with tender consciences and penitential tears they mourned because of their transgressions. But as this day was a festival, a day of holy convocation, a day which the Lord had commanded to be kept with joy and gladness, they were bidden by their teachers to restrain their grief, and to rejoice in view of the great mercy of God toward them. "For," Nehemiah said, "this day is holy unto our Lord; neither be ye sorry; for the joy of the Lord is your strength."

Accordingly, after the earlier part of the day had been devoted to religious exercises, the people spent the remainder in gratefully recounting the blessings of God, and enjoying the bounties which he had granted them, remembering also to send portions to the poor who had nothing to prepare. And there was great rejoicing, because they understood the words of the law which had been declared to them. The work of reading and expounding the law to the people was continued upon the following day. The solemn services of the day of atonement were performed at the time appointed,—on the tenth day of the seventh month,—according to the command of God. And from the fifteenth to the twenty-second of the same month the people and the rulers kept once more the feast of tabernacles.

It was published "in all their cities, and in Jerusalem, saying, Go forth unto the mount, and fetch olive branches, and pine branches, and myrtle branches, and palm branches, and branches of thick trees, to make booths, as it is written. So the people went forth, and brought them, and made themselves booths, every one upon the roof of his house, and in their courts, and in the courts of the house of God.... And all the congregation of them that were come again out of the captivity made booths, and sat under the booths; for since the days of Joshua the son of Nun unto that day had not the children of Israel done so. And there was very great gladness. Also day by day, from the first day unto the last day, he [Ezra] read in the book of the law of God."

—*Southern Watchman, May 31, 1904*

Chapter 15

A Solemn Fast

When the Feast of Tabernacles was past, one day only having intervened, the children of Israel kept a solemn fast. This was held not merely at the command of the rulers, but by the desire of the people. As they had from day to day listened to the words of the law, they had been deeply convicted of their own transgressions, and also of the sins of their nation in past generations. They saw that it was because of their departure from God that his protecting care had been withdrawn from them, and they had been scattered in foreign lands. And they now determined to seek God's mercy and to pledge themselves to walk hereafter in his commandments.

Before entering upon the services of the day, they carefully separated themselves from the heathen who were intermingled with them. This being done, "they stood up in their place, and read in the book of the law of the Lord their God one fourth part of the day; and another fourth part they confessed, and worshiped the Lord their God."

The people prostrated themselves before the Lord, humbly confessing their sins and pleading for mercy and pardon, each for himself individually, and for the entire congregation. Then their leaders encouraged them to believe that God, according to his promise had heard their prayers. They showed them that they were not only to mourn and weep and repent of their transgressions, but to trust that God had pardoned them, and to evince their faith by recounting his mercies and praising him for his goodness. Said these teachers, "Stand up and bless the Lord your God forever and ever."

Then from the gathered throng, as they stood with hands outstretched toward heaven, arose the song of praise and adoration: "Blessed be thy glorious name, which is exalted above all blessing and praise. Thou, even thou, art Lord alone; thou hast made heaven, the heaven of heavens, with all their host, the earth, and all things that are therein, the seas, and all that is therein; and thou preservest them all, and the host of heaven worshipeth thee."

In this portion of sacred history is a precious lesson of faith for all who are convicted of sin, and weighed down with a sense of their unworthiness. When they compare their characters with God's great standard of right, they see themselves condemned as transgressors. There is no power in law to free them from their guilt. But as they confess their sins, they can find pardon through Christ. From him flows the cleansing stream that can wash away the stains of sin. When the sinner has come to Christ with contrition of soul, confessing his transgressions, it is then his duty to appropriate to himself the Saviour's promise of pardon to the repentant and believing. He who seeks to find goodness and cause for rejoicing in himself, will always be in despair; but he who looks to Jesus, the author and finisher of his faith, can say with confidence, "I live, yet not I, but Christ liveth in me."

Following the song of praise, the leaders of the congregation presented the history of Israel, showing God's great benefits and their ingratitude. Tracing the record from the days of Abraham, they called attention to God's design to preserve his name upon the earth by preserving for himself a people pure amid the general corruption; they recounted the mighty manifestations of his power in their deliverance from bondage in Egypt, and showed also how backsliding and apostasy had caused the blessing of the Lord to be withdrawn from Israel. Then the whole congregation entered into a covenant to keep all the commandments of God; and that the transaction might be as effectual as possible, this covenant was written out, and those who were thoroughly in earnest in the work of reformation affixed their names and seals. They wished to preserve for future reference a memorial of the obligation they had just taken upon themselves, as a reminder of duty and a barrier against temptation. Thus it was that the people took a solemn oath to "walk in God's law, which was given by Moses the servant of God, and to observe and do all the commandments of the Lord our Lord, and his judgments and his statutes." The oath taken also included a promise not to intermarry with "the people of the land." This had often been done by the people; and sometimes the rulers, as Solomon, and Ahab, had formed such unions; and these marriages, by introducing idolatry, had resulted in the ruin of thousands.

The Lord had strictly forbidden the intermarrying of his people with other nations. This would prevent the Hebrews from marrying idolaters, and thus forming connections with heathen families. The reason which God assigned for prohibiting these marriages was, "They will turn away thy son from following me." But the heathen were less guilty than are the impenitent in this age, who, having the light of the gospel, persistently refuse to accept it. Those among ancient Israel who ventured to disregard the divine prohibition, did it at the sacrifice of religious principle. When those who now profess to be God's people join themselves in marriage with the ungodly, they form a tie uniting them to the world, and they will probably soon be one with them, notwithstanding their present profession.

Before the day of fasting ended, the people still further manifested their determination to return unto the Lord. With one accord, all pledged themselves to cease the desecration of the Sabbath. Nehemiah did not at this time, as at a later date, exercise his authority to prevent heathen traders from coming into Jerusalem on the Sabbath, for the sale of provisions and other articles; but to save the people from yielding to temptation, he engaged them, by a solemn covenant, not to transgress the Sabbath law by purchasing of those vendors, hoping that this would discourage them, and put an end to their traffic.

Provision was also made to support the public worship of God. A pledge was given by the congregation to contribute yearly a stated sum for the service of the sanctuary, as well as to bring the tithes and the "first-fruits of our ground, and the first-fruits of all fruit of all trees, year by year, unto the house of the Lord; also the first-born of our sons, and of our cattle, as it is written in the law, and the firstlings of our herds and of our flocks, to bring to the house of our God."

The liberality of the Jews in their offerings for religious purposes might well be imitated by Christians. If tithes and offerings were required thousands of years ago, they are much more essential now. The labors of God's servants were then confined almost wholly to the land of Palestine; but the apostles and their successors were commissioned to preach the gospel throughout the world. The people of this dispensation are favored with greater light and blessing than were the Jews; therefore they are placed under even greater obligation to honor God and to advance his cause.

The efforts of Nehemiah to restore the worship of the true God had been crowned with success. If Israel would be true to the oath they had taken, a bright future was before them; for the Lord has always magnified his law before his people, pouring rich blessings upon them so long as they have been obedient. The history of God's ancient people is full of instruction for the church of today. While the Bible faithfully presents the results of their apostasy as a warning to all future generations, it portrays, as a worthy example, the deep humiliation and repentance, the earnest devotion and generous sacrifice, that marked their seasons of returning to the Lord. There is encouragement, too, in the record of God's willingness to receive his backsliding but repentant people. It would be a scene well-pleasing to God and angels, would his professed followers in this generation unite, as did Israel of old, in a solemn covenant to "observe and do all the commandments of the Lord our Lord, and his judgments and his statutes."

—Southern Watchman, June 7, 1904

Chapter 16

A Sabbath Reformation

Under the labors of Ezra and Nehemiah, the people of Judah had in the most solemn and public manner pledged themselves to render obedience to the law of God. But when the influence of these teachers was for a time withdrawn, there were many who departed from the Lord. During the absence of Nehemiah from Jerusalem, idolaters not only gained a foothold in the city, but contaminated by their presence the very precincts of the temple. Certain families of Israel, having intermarried with the family of Tobiah the Ammonite, had brought about a friendship between this man, one of Judah's most bitter and determined enemies, and Eliashib the high priest. As a result of this unhallowed alliance, Tobiah had been permitted to occupy a commodious apartment connected with the temple, which had been devoted to the storing of various offerings brought for the service of God.

Thus not only was the temple of the Lord profaned, but his people were constantly exposed to the corrupting influence of this agent of Satan. Because of their cruelty and treachery toward Israel, the Ammonites and Moabites had by the word of the Lord been forever excluded from the congregation. And yet, in defiance of this solemn edict, the high priest himself casts out the consecrated oblations from the chamber of God's house, to make a place for the most violent and treacherous of a proscribed people. Greater contempt for God could not have been manifested than was expressed in this favor conferred on this enemy of God and his truth.

When Nehemiah learned of this bold profanation, he promptly exercised his authority to expel the intruder. "It grieved me sore; therefore I cast forth all the household stuff of Tobiah out of the chamber. Then I commanded, and they cleansed the chambers; and thither brought I again the vessels of the house of God, with the meat offering and the frankincense."

Not only had the temple been profaned, but the offerings had been misapplied. This tended to discourage the liberality of the people. They lost their zeal and fervor in the cause of God, and were reluctant to pay their tithes. The treasuries of the Lord's house were but poorly supplied; and the singers and others employed in the temple service not receiving a sufficient support, many left the work of God to labor elsewhere for the maintenance of their families. Nehemiah promptly corrected these abuses. He gathered together those who had forsaken the service of the house of God, and caused the tithes and offerings to be restored. Faithful men were appointed to take charge of the means raised, confidence was restored, and all Judah brought their tithes to the treasuries of the Lord.

Another result of intercourse with idolaters was disregard of the Sabbath. Heathen merchants and traders from the surrounding country had been intent upon leading the children of Israel to engage in traffic upon the Sabbath. While there were some who would not be induced to sacrifice principle, and transgress the commandment of God, others were more easily influenced, and joined with the heathen in their endeavor to overcome the scruples of their more conscientious countrymen; and the idolaters boasted of the success that had attended their efforts. Many dared openly to violate the Sabbath. While some engaged in traffic with the heathen, others were treading in wine presses, and others bringing in sheaves upon the Sabbath day.

Had the rulers exerted their influence and exercised their authority, this state of things might have been prevented; but their desire to advance their own secular interest led them to favor the ungodly. It is mingling our interest with the interest of unbelievers that leads to apostasy and the ruin of the soul.

Nehemiah rebuked them for their shameful neglect of duty, which was largely responsible for the fast-spreading apostasy. "What evil thing is this that ye do, and profane the Sabbath day?" he sternly demanded. "Did not your fathers thus, and did not our God bring all this evil upon us, and upon this city? yet ye bring more wrath upon Israel by profaning the Sabbath." He gave command that when it "began to be dark before the Sabbath," the city gates should be shut, and that they should not be opened till the Sabbath was past; and, having more confidence in his own servants than in those the magistrates of Jerusalem might appoint, he stationed them at the gate to see that his orders were enforced.

The merchants were not disposed to abandon their purpose; and several times they lodged without the gates of the city, hoping to find opportunity for traffic, either with citizens or country people. Upon being informed of this, Nehemiah warned them that they would be punished if they continued this practice. He also directed the Levites to guard the gates, knowing that on account of their higher position they would command greater respect than the common people; while from their close connection with the service of God, it was reasonable to expect that they would be more zealous in enforcing obedience to his law.

—Southern Watchman, June 29, 1904

Chapter 17

The Sacredness of God's Law

By the observance of the Sabbath the Israelites were to be distinguished from all other nations as the worshipers of the true God, the Creator of the heavens and the earth. The Sabbath was the divinely-appointed memorial of the creative work, and the day upon which it was to be celebrated was not left indefinite. It was not any day which men might choose and no day in particular, but the very day in which the Creator rested, that was sanctified and hallowed. On this day God would come very near to his obedient, commandment-loving people.

God places a very high estimate upon his law. Moses and Joshua commanded that it be read publicly at stated periods, that all the people might be familiar with its precepts, and reduce them to practice. If they did this, they had the exalted privilege of being counted as sons and daughters of the Most High, and might confide in him as dear children. In Nehemiah's day, the adversary of souls, working through the children of disobedience, and taking advantage of the unfaithfulness of men in holy office, was fast lulling the nation to forgetfulness of God's law, the very sin which had provoked his wrath against their fathers; and for a time it seemed that all the care, labor, and expense involved in rebuilding the defenses of Jerusalem would be lost.

David prayed, "It is time for thee, Lord, to work: for they have made void thy law." This prayer is no less pertinent at the present time. The world has gone astray from God, and its lawless state should strike terror to the heart, and lead all who are loyal to the great King to work for a reformation. The papal power has thought to change the law of God by substituting a spurious Sabbath for that of Jehovah; and all through the religious world the false Sabbath is revered, while the true one is trampled beneath unholy feet. But will the Lord degrade his law to meet the standard of finite man? Will he accept a day possessing no sanctity, in the place of his own Sabbath, which he has hallowed and blessed?—No; it is on the law of God that the last great struggle of the controversy between Christ and his angels and Satan and his angels will come, and it will be decisive for all the world. This is the hour of temptation to God's people; but Daniel saw them delivered out of it, every one whose name is written in the Lamb's book of life.

Men in responsible positions will not only ignore and despise the Sabbath themselves, but from the sacred desk will urge upon the people the observance of the first day of the week, pleading tradition and custom in behalf of this manmade institution. They will point to calamities on land and sea—to the storms of wind, the floods, the earthquakes, the destruction by fire—as judgments indicating God's displeasure because Sunday is not sacredly observed. These calamities will increase more and more, one disaster will follow close upon the heels of another; and those who make void the law of God will point to the few who are keeping the Sabbath of the forth commandment as the ones who are bringing wrath upon the world. This falsehood is Satan's device that he may ensnare the unwary.

We need Nehemiahs in this age of the world, who shall arouse the people to see how far from God they are because of the transgression of his law. Nehemiah was a reformer, a great man raised up for an important time. As he came in contact with evil and every kind of opposition, fresh courage and zeal were aroused. His energy and determination inspired the people of Jerusalem; and strength and courage took the place of feebleness and discouragement. His holy purpose, his high hope, his cheerful consecration to the work, were contagious. The people caught the enthusiasm of their leader, and in his sphere each man became a Nehemiah, and helped to make stronger the hand and heart of his neighbor. Here is a lesson for ministers of the present day. If they are listless, inactive, destitute of godly zeal, what can be expected of the people to whom they minister?

Man's personal accountability to God should command careful attention. The law can never pardon. Its province is not to save the transgressor, but to convict him. It is far-reaching, and all we do bears the stamp of its approval or condemnation. Men professing godliness often regard the secret sins of the soul very lightly; but it is the secret motives of the heart that determine the true character, and God will bring them into judgment. The dangers resulting from disobeying God and seeking the friendship of the world have not lessened with the lapse of time. There is earnest work to be done; and the faithful watchman, who is actuated by love to God and a desire to save sinners, will reap the reward of his labors; but the unfaithful watchman, whose influence tends to union with the world, will cause the ruin of many souls.

—*Southern Watchman, June 24, 1904*

Chapter 18

Separation of Israel from Idolaters

Another subject to which Nehemiah's attention was called on his return to Jerusalem, was the danger that threatened Israel from intermarriage and association with idolaters. "In those days also," says Nehemiah, "saw I Jews that had married wives of Ashdod, of Ammon, and of Moab; and their children spake half in the speech of

Ashdod, and could not speak in the Jews' language, but according to the language of each people." This assimilation to the language of the heathen was an indication of the inroads made by heathenism. In many families, children, trained by heathen mothers, were prattling around them in the tongue of the several idolatrous nations with whom the Israelites had intermarried. These children, as they grew up in the habits and customs of heathenism, became idolaters of the most dangerous class, because they were connected with the people of God.

These unlawful alliances caused great confusion; for some who entered into them were persons in high position, rulers of the people and men connected with the service of God, to whom, in the absence of Nehemiah, the people had a right to look for counsel and correct example. God had carefully excluded the heathen from uniting with his faithful worshipers; but the divinely, erected barriers had been broken down, and as a consequence of mingling and intermarrying with other nations, the Israel of God were fast losing their peculiar, holy character.

Nehemiah knew that ruin was before the nation if this evil were not put away, and he reasoned with these men on the subject. He firmly and fearlessly declared, "Ye shall not give your daughters unto their sons, nor take their daughters unto your sons, or for yourselves." He presented the case of Solomon, and reminded them that among many nations there had arisen no king like this man, whom God had favored, and to whom he had given great wisdom. But the idolatrous women whom he connected with his house by marriage, led his heart astray from God, and his example had a corrupting influence on all Israel.

The commands and threatenings of the Lord, and the fearful judgments visited upon Israel in past generations, aroused the consciences of the people. The strongest and most endearing ties that bound them to idolaters were broken. Not only were future marriages with the heathen forbidden, but marriages already formed were dissolved.

Some men in sacred office pleaded for their heathen wives, declaring that they could not bring themselves to separate from them. Nehemiah replied, with solemn sternness, "Shall we then hearken unto you to do all this great evil, to transgress against our God in marrying strange wives?"

A grandson of the high priest, having married a daughter of the notorious Sanballat, was not only removed from office, but promptly banished from Israel. "Remember them, O my God," exclaimed Nehemiah, "because they have defiled the priesthood, and the covenant of the priesthood, and of the Levites." He adds: "Thus cleansed I them from all strangers, and appointed the wards of the priests and the Levites, every one in his business." No respect was shown for rank or position. No distinction was made. Whoever among the priests and rulers refused to sever his connection with idolaters, was immediately separated from the service of the Lord.

How much anguish of soul this needed severity cost the faithful workers for God, the Judgment alone will reveal. Every advance step was gained only by fasting, humiliation, and prayer. There was a constant struggle with opposing elements.

Many who had married idolaters chose to go with them into exile; and, with those who had been expelled from the congregation, they joined the Samaritans, a heathen people who had combined with their idolatrous worship many of the customs of the Jews. Hither some who had occupied high positions in the work of God now found their way, and after a time they cast in their lot fully with them. Desiring to strengthen this alliance, the Samaritans promised to adopt more fully the Jewish faith and customs; and the apostates, determined to outdo their former brethren, erected a temple on Mount Gerizim, in opposition to the house of God at Jerusalem. This spurious religion continued to be a mixture of Judaism and heathenism; and their claims to be the people of God were the source of schism, emulation, and enmity between the two nations from generation to generation.

—Southern Watchman, July 5, 1904

Chapter 19

The Need of True Reformers

The servants of God today encounter difficulties very similar to those against which Nehemiah contended. Human nature is still the same. And Satan is as active, earnest, and persevering now as at any period in the past. Nay, rather, the word of God declares that his power and enmity increase as we near the close of time. The greatest danger of God's ancient people arose from their inclination to disregard his direct requirements and to follow, instead, their own desires. Such is the sin and danger of his people at the present time. The indolence, backsliding, and degeneracy in our churches may be traced, in a great degree, to the lax sentiments which have been coming in as a result of conformity to the world. The Sabbath is not as sacredly regarded as it should be. Improper marriages, with their train of evils, have dragged down some of the useful men to apostasy and ruin.

Before contracting marriage, every wise person will consider the matter in all its bearings: "Will the relation I am about to form lead heavenward, or toward perdition? Will it bring in sacred and devotional influences, or the corrupting influence of the world?"

In the existing state of religious declension, there is crying need of earnest, faithful Nehemiahs and Ezras,—men who will not shun to call sin by its right name, and who will not shrink from vindicating the honor of God. Those upon whom God has laid the burden of his work are not to hold their peace, and cover prevailing evils with a cloak of false charity.

Men of courage and energy are needed to expose fashionable sins. Iniquity must not be palliated and excused. Those who lead the church to follow the customs and practices of the world, are not to be lauded and exalted. No regard for family or position will hinder the faithful servants of Christ from guarding the interests of his people. God is no respecter of persons. Great light and special privileges bring increased responsibility. When those who have been favored or honored of God commit sin, their influence goes very far to encourage others in transgression. And if, by their example, the faith of another is weakened, and moral and religious principle is broken down, the wrath of God will surely come upon those betrayers of their sacred trust.

Severity to a few will often prove mercy to many. Yet we must be careful to manifest the spirit of Christ, and not our own hasty, impetuous disposition. We must rebuke sin, because we love God, and love the souls for whom Christ died.

Ezra and Nehemiah repeatedly humbled themselves before God, confessing the sins of their people, and entreating pardon as if they themselves were the offenders. Patiently they toiled and prayed and suffered, because of the disaffection of those who should have joined with them, but whose sympathies were more frequently with their adversaries. That which rendered their work most difficult and trying was not the open hostility of the heathen without, but the secret opposition of traitors in the camp, and even among the priests and rulers. By lending their talents and influence to the service of evil-workers, these men of divided hearts increased tenfold the burden of God's faithful servants. They furnished the Lord's enemies with material to use in their warfare upon his people. Evil passions and rebellious wills were ever at war with the plain and direct requirements of God.

The spirit of true reform will be met in our day as in ancient times. Those who are zealous for the honor of God, and who will not countenance sin either in ministers or people, need not expect rest or pleasure in this life. Untiring vigilance must be the watchword of all who guard the interests of Christ's church. During Nehemiah's absence from Jerusalem, evils were introduced which threatened to pervert the nation.

The same dangers exist in our time. If those who have the oversight of the church leave their charge, unconsecrated ones, claiming to believe the truth but having no connection with God, will take advantage of their absence to do much harm. The restraint Being removed from these self-seeking and turbulent spirits, their peculiar traits of character are made prominent, and by their hints, insinuations, and deceptive charges, they create doubt, unbelief, and dissension among the Lord's people. Such forget that spiritual things are spiritually discerned. They judge of the character and motives of God's servants according to their own ignorance of truth and the ways of righteousness. Their example, words, and influence weaken the force of God's requirements, and divide and scatter the church of Christ.

The word of God abounds in sharp and striking contrasts. Sin and holiness are placed side by side, that, beholding, we may hate and shun the one, and love and embrace the other. The pages that describe the hatred, falsehood, and treachery of a Sanballat or a Tobiah, describe also the nobility, devotion, and self-sacrifice of a Nehemiah or an Ezra. We are left free to copy either as we choose.

The fearful results of transgressing God's commandments are placed over against the blessings resulting from obedience thereto. We ourselves are to decide whether we will suffer the one or enjoy the other. The law of God remains unchanged. Like himself, it is pure, perfect, and eternal. It is not enough to profess to be keepers of the law. The question is, Are we carrying out its principles in our daily life? "Righteousness exalteth a nation; but sin is a reproach to any people." Saith the voice of wisdom: "Receive my instruction, and not silver; and knowledge rather than choice gold. For wisdom is better than rubies; and all the things that may be desired are not to be compared to it."

—Southern Watchman, July 12, 1904

Other books by TEACH Services, Inc.

1844 Vol. 1–3   *Jerome L. Clark* $29.95
These volumes go forth in the hope that it will give the reader a deeper
insight into the atmosphere of reform which permeated the time in which
arose the Millerite Movement, the seedbed of the Seventh-day Adventist
Church. Such an atmosphere made people receptive to change and
provided the attitude of mind which made the widespread dissemination
of new ideas possible. Surely it was in the providence of God that the
"great Second Advent Movement" arose at such a time.

Absolutely Vegetarian   *Lorine Tadej* . . . . $ 8.95
A complete guide to maintaining a strict vegetarian lifestyle. A way to
reach your ideal weight and maintain it, as long as you live.

Activated Charcoal   *David Cooney* . . . . $ 7.95
This publication represents an attempt to gather together most of what
has been reported to date on the use of activated charcoal as an oral
antidote and as a remedy for other ailments.

Adam's Table   *Reggi Burnett* . . . . $ 8.95
A cookbook to help the user obtain optimum healthier and happier
lifestyle through changes in their cooking style. Originated from Adam's
Table Restaurant in Albuquerque, NM.

An Adventure in Cooking   *Joanne Chitwood Nowack* $12.95
This book has been compiled especially to teach young people, in a
step-by-step, progressive way, the art of vegetarian cookery. Cooking is
a real art, and very practical one too, since we need to eat every day.

The Antichrist 666   *William Josiah Sutton* . . . . $ 8.95
Positive proof for Bible Believing People: Who the beast is; Who his
image is; What the mark of the beast is; How to count the number of the
beast. Edited by Roy Allan Anderson, D.D.

The Anti-Christ Exposed   *Dan Jarrard* . . . . $ 5.95
A biblical and historical study of the counterfeit religious system which
is against God and His people.

Caring Kitchen Recipes   *Gloria Lawson* $12.95
Specializes in recipes for better health that features: whole grains, vegetarian, dairy-free and nourishing dessert recipes.

The Celtic Church in Britain   *Leslie Hardinge* . . . . $ 8.95
This is an authoritative study of the beliefs and practice of the Celtic
Church which at the same time holds much interest for the non-specialist,
containing as it does fascinating descriptions of the life of the early Celtic
Christians in their monastic walled villages modelled on the Old Testa-
ment cities of refuge. Their elaborate penitential discipline was based on
Old Testament compensatory regulations. Obedience to the Scriptures
led them to establish a remarkable theocracy based on the laws of the
Pentateuch and including the keeping of the Seventh-day Sabbath.

Children's Bible Lessons *Bessie White* .... $ 3.95
These seven Children's Bible Lessons are prepared for use during
Evangelistic Meetings, Bible seminars, Vacation Bible Schools, or at the
Church's discretion.

Christian Faith & Religious Freedom *Olsen, V.N.* .... $ 8.95
The theological grounding provided in this book is an important antidote
to the tendency of many to base their arguments on religious freedom
and church/state issues on political or constitutional grounds. Dr. Olsen
makes an important contribution to our thinking by making us face the
theological bedrock of any Christian approach to these topics.

Convert's Catechism *Peter Geiermann* .... $ 2.50
The quoted statement on changing solemnity from Saturday to Sunday
can be found in this reproduction.

Cooking With Natural Foods I *Muriel Beltz* $14.95
An ideal eating program for a preventive lifestyle, weight control and
stress control. A program designed to give an alternative in the prevention
and treatment of disease.

Country Life Natural Foods Something Better Cookbook $14.95
This cookbook was originally designed to be used as a reference book in
local community vegetarian cooking schools given across the country.
Persons interested in better education in general health principles, and
wholesome vegetarian recipes will find this cookbook a treasure to read,
use and share. Completely revised and updated.

Divine Philosophy & Science of Health & Healing *Paulien* ... $19.95
All of the principles of the Bible and the Spirit of Prophecy are designed
to allow us to function in perfect harmony with God Himself. This book
discusses the methods and means of healthful living. It deals with going
back to First Things, and relying by faith upon the substances which God
has established for our benefit.

Don't Drink Your Milk *Frank Oski, MD* .... $ 7.95
Dr. Oski, the head of Pediatrics at Johns Hopkins University School of
Medicine, gives the frightening new medical facts about the world's most
overrated nutrient.

Dove of Gold *Leslie Hardinge* .... $ 7.95
This book approaches the vast subject of the Holy Spirit viewing His
functions through illustrations He himself has selected as vehicles for the
revelation of His character and work. As one observes the related aspects
of the nature and function of the natural object used as a symbol, the work
of the Holy Spirit will become clearer, and His disposition of concern
and affection much more appealing.

Earthly Life of Jesus *Ken LeBrun* $19.95
Biblical accounts of each event in Christ's earthly life carefully arranged
together from the KJV Bible. Words of Jesus in red with full index.

Fire Bell in the Night   *Ralph Moss* . . . . $ 5.95
News items and stories from both the secular press and from religious
newspapers, along with journals and articles by secular and religious
authors will be linked with Bible prophecy to reveal a most startling
scenario in just the last few years, and to lay a case to expose an
undreamed of enemy who is rapidly winning the confidence of most of
this world's inhabitants.

From Eden to Eden   *J. H. Waggoner* . . . . $ 9.95
A most interesting study of the more important historic and prophetic
portions of the Scriptures.

Garlic—Nature's Perfect Prescription   Hullquist, MD . . . . $ 9.95
Garlic, the Lily of Legend, has today become the focus of modern
medical research. Recognized for thousands of years for its amazing
curative powers, this bulb is today not only known for its potent bouquet
but is drawing the attention of the scientific world as a potential antibiotic,
anticancer, antioxidant, anti-aging, anti-inflammatory…the list goes on
and on.

God's Justice—Administered in Love   *Dick Beman* . . . . $ 5.95
You can learn the secret of how to stand firm in the Judgment, without
being afraid, and yet maintain a healthy, respectful fear of God.

Gospel In Creation   *E. J. Waggoner*. . . . . $ 6.95
This book directs our wandering gaze to the open pages of God's created
works as the expression of the gospel, the power of God to save from sin.
Facsimile Reprint.

Grandma Whitney   *Wm. Andress & Winnie Gohde*. . . . . $ 8.95
At 91, Hulda Crooks gained international acclaim by becoming the oldest
woman to climb Mt. Fuji, Japan's tallest mountain. Six weeks later she
broke her own record as the oldest person to climb Mt. Whitney. This is
her story.

Healing By God's Natural Methods   *Al. Wolfsen* . . . . $ 4.95
Al. Wolfsen has taught hundreds of sick people how to use only simple,
non-poisonous remedies.

Healthful Living   *Ellen G. White* $10.95
Wherever this book has been received, it has been recognized as a
veritable storehouse of seed thoughts relating to the great practical
themes with which it deals. Facsimile Reprint.

Healthy Food Choices   *Leona R. Alderson*. $14.95
Some special features include: guidelines for menu planning, breakfast
suggestions, ideas for brown bag lunches, and much more!

Helps to Bible Study   *J. L. Shuler*. . . . . $ 2.95
A Bible marking system which contains Bible studies covering twenty-
eight topics including "The Second Coming," "The Seal of the Living
God," "Bible Temperance," and "Christian in Dress." It is simple and
practical in its approach, and will benefit all ages.

Holy Spirit Seminar *Harold Penninger* . . . . $ 7.95
A collection of Holy Spirit Seminars for study, inspiration, etc.

Hydrotherapy—Simple Treatments *Thomas/Dail* . . . . $ 8.95
Help your body overcome common diseases using hydrotherapy and
simple home treatments.

The Illuminati 666 *William Josiah Sutton* . . . . $ 8.95
Find out about the Illuminati, its startling history, and how powerful it
has become. Includes a study of the origins of false religions, and the
forms they are taking today. Introduction by Roy Allan Anderson, D.D.

Incredible Edibles *Eriann Hullquist* . . . . $ 7.95
Some "health" meals taste bland, some are hard to make, others require
strange or hard to find ingredients. Eriann has developed a simple method
of meal preparation where each recipe looks good and tastes great.

The Justified Walk *Frank Phillips* . . . . $ 8.95
Before you can rightly tackle a problem, you must first be able to clearly
understand its nature. Before you can discuss it with others, you must
first define your terms. In this book Elder Phillips makes clear how the
plan of salvation works in our daily lives. Faith, Grace, Sin, Justification,
Sanctification and Righteousness are made real and tangible.

Lessons On Faith *Jones & Waggoner* . . . . $ 6.95
This is a compilation of articles and sermons given in the 1890's by Jones
and Waggoner on Righteousness By Faith.

Let the Holy Spirit Speak *Garrie Fraser Williams* . . . . $ 4.95
A remarkable new book that is not just a study guide but a unique resource
of Bible study methods and small group information.

Letters to the Churches *M. L. Andreasen* . . . . $ 7.95
A collection of letters objecting to statements in the book *SDA's Answer
to Questions on Doctrine*. Andreasen was Conference President, President of Union College, and Secretary at the General Conference.

Living the Life of Enoch *E. G. White* . . . . $ 7.95
We are to live the Enoch life! This is our commission. and this is a twofold
work—to develop a character of righteousness by living a life of personal
purity and pleading with God; to teach a lesson of godliness by kindly
acts and warning and pleading with men.

Living Fountains or Broken Cisterns *E. A. Sutherland* $12.95
This book tells how we should set up our education systems to follow
the heavenly blueprint. The goal is to have the best Christian schools in
the world.

Manners *Paloma Chalker* $12.95
Here is help for Christian parents who want their children to know that
good manners never go out of style. You will find this book a good,
old-fashioned approach to behavior.

Mystical Medicine *Warren Peters* . . . . $ 7.95
Many people today have come to believe that our modern, technological
system of health care in the Western world isn't proving to be the great
boon that it was once thought to be. Frustrated and disillusioned people
are turning to "more natural" methods of treatment. As we become aware
of the intimate connection between the physical, mental and spiritual
aspects of our nature, we are flocking to holistic medicine by the
thousands.

National Sunday Law *A. T. Jones* . . . . $ 7.95
This book is a report of an argument made concerning the national
Sunday bill that was introduced by Senator Blair in the fiftieth Congress.

Nature's Banquet *Living Springs* $12.95
Cooking is an Art and a Science. You will find that the art and science
of cooking is especially enjoyable when using natural foods and when
learning to be a vegetarian cook. The art of food preparation will give
you the opportunity to exercise your enlightened preference and your
personality to create attractive, delicious and nutritious meals. The
science of cooking involves techniques and properties of food which
affect its successful preparation.

Nutrition Workshop Guide *Eriann Hullquist* . . . . 10 for $ 9.95
Chock full of nutritional recipes, as well as lots of helpful nutritional tips
for special situations, such as road trips, fast foods, etc.

Now! *Merikay McLeod* . . . . $ .99
This book written by a 17 year old girl, graphically portrays a possible
end-time scenario. It is a heart warming and thrilling account of God's
protection and care of His people, and the trials, triumphs, and joy that
lie ahead for them.

Pioneer Stories *Arthur W. Spalding* . . . . $ 9.95
It is good for children to know what their fathers and mothers did; for
sometimes that makes a pattern of what the children should do. Especially
is this true if the children are set to finish the work their parents began.
And that is the reason why this book is written, to tell the children of the
pioneers in the second advent movement the beginnings of that movement, and reasons why they are to carry it on.

Place of Herbs in Rational Therapy *D. E. Robinson* . . . . $ .90
Quotations relative to the use of herbs in therapy from D. E. Robinson,
who was the secretary to Mrs. White.

Power of Prayer *E. G. White* . . . . $ 7.95
Prayer is our connection with God—our strength, our bridge to heaven!
As we pray, the Holy Spirit Himself unites in our petitions and "maketh
intercession for us." We are not alone in our battle of life; all heaven is
on our side!

Preparation For Translation *Milton Crane*................ $ 7.95
This book is about YOUR preparation for translation. It is about YOUR
plans to live without a mediator after probation closes. It is about God's
plans for YOUR overcoming temptation NOW in anticipation of those
events. It is about His plans for the renewing of YOUR mind through the
final atonement ministry of Jesus. Spanish editions—$8.95.

Principles To Live By *Mel Rees*.......................... $ 4.95
Dominion calls for individual decision and action—therefore, God gave
man guiding principles to live by.

Quick-n-Easy Natural Recipes *Lorrie Knutsen* .... $ 2.95
Every recipe has five or fewer ingredients and most take only minutes to
prepare. Now you can enjoy simple, natural recipes without the drudgery!

Raw Food Treatment of Cancer *Kristine Nolfi, MD*.......... $ 3.95
This book tells of the importance of raw vegetables in the diet of healing
and general good health. Dr. Nolfi was a physician in Denmark for over
50 years.

Returning Back to Eden *Betty-Ann Peters*.................. $ 9.95
These recipes have been taste-tested by the world-wide travelers that
have visited the Back to Eden Restaurant & Bakery in Minocqua, WI.

Rome's Challenge *Catholic Mirror* .... $ .99
"The pages of this brochure unfold to the reader one of the most glaringly
conceivable contradictions existing between the practice and theory of
the Protestant world, and unsusceptible of any rational solution, the
theory claiming the Bible alone as the teacher.

The Sabbath *M. L. Andreasen*............................ $ 9.95
Attacks upon the Sabbath throughout the ages have been numerous and
persistent, and they have all been grounded upon human reasoning as as
against the command of God. Men can see no reason why any other day
than one commanded by God is not just as good. Men cannot see why
one day in seven is not just as good as the seventh day. The answer, of
course, is that the difference lies in God's command. It is at this point
that man's reason sets aside a positive command of God. It is not merely
a question of this or that day, but the greater question of obedience to
God's command.

Shadows of His Sacrifice *Leslie Hardinge* .... $ 7.95
Understanding Jesus through the types and symbols of the Sanctuary.
God has given us the details of the sanctuary so we can study each part
minutely. Only then will we be able to see Christ in His fullness. Jesus
is the Sacrifice. He is also the priest. He is the Shekinah, and He is also
the veil. He is "every whit!"

Solemn Appeal   *Ellen G. White* . . . . $ 5.95
Contains articles by Ellen G. White which appeared in the book *A Solemn Appeal Relative to the Solitary Vice and Abuses and Excesses of the Marriage Relation*, published in 1870 by the Stream press of Battle Creek. Articles include: "Appeal to Mothers," The Marriage Relationship," Obedience to the Law of God," "Female Modesty," and "Sentimentalism."

Steps To Christ Study Guide   *Gail Bremner* . . . . $ 2.95
This study guide is designed to encourage the youth, and the young at heart, to understand and experience more fully a living relationship with Jesus.

Story of Daniel the Prophet   *S. N. Haskell* $11.95
This book especially applicable to our day: points out the immediate future and in its simplicity will attract many who might not be inclined to read deep, argumentative works. Facsimile Reprint.

Story of the Seer of Patmos   *S. N. Haskell* $12.95
The Book of Revelation pronounces a blessing upon everyone who reads it or hears it. Facsimile Reprint.

Stress: Taming the Tyrant   *Richard Neil* . . . . $ 8.95
Stress is an inevitable part of our 20th century lifestyle. Under the proper circumstances stress can be uplifting as well as depressing. It can either help us grow our hasten or death. Find out how to control, manage and modify stress.

Studies in Daniel and Revelation   *Kraid Ashbaugh* . . . . $ 4.95
A convenient handbook containing paraphrases of EG White's comments after each verse in the books of Daniel & Revelation.

Studies in the Book of Hebrews   *E. J. Waggoner* . . . . $ 6.95
A series of studies given at the General Conference of 1897. The Bible studies that Elder Waggoner gave each day, are presented as live and full of hope for each Bible student today.

Subtle Challenge to God's Authority   *Milton Crane* . . . . $ 5.50
Satan's deceptions are many and subtle. He has concentrated his attack on God's authority.

Such A Cloud of Witnesses   *Milton Crane* . . . . $ 4.95
You are called to be a witness for or against the government of God. Will your testimony help God or aid His enemy?

375 Meatless Recipes–CENTURY 21   *Ethel Nelson, MD* . . . . . . $ 7.95
This book will help you learn how to feed your family in such a way that they will enjoy eating the foods that nutritionists tell us are an absolute must if we are going to make it into the twenty-first century.

Truth Triumphant   *B. G. Wilkinson* $12.95
The history of God's true Church from Ireland, to the Waldenses, the struggle to preserve the Bible and the pure doctrine of the apostles is disclosed. Facsimile Reprint.

Understanding the Body Organs   *Celeste Lee* . . . . $ 7.95
Simply and concisely explains how the body organs function and how they relate to one another. Also includes the eight laws of health, explaining each one and sharing many benefits that will be derived from following the entire plan.

Vegetarian Cooking School Cookbook   *Vierra* $11.95
Medical doctors and scientists are just now discovering a wealth of new facts about fruits and vegetables, and their findings are amazing. These foods contain high amounts of antioxidant nutrients and phytochemicals that not only nourish the body and build the immune system, but they prevent cancer…This unique cookbook contains over 170 of the tastiest vegetarian recipes as well as many facts and charts supporting why it is wise to avoid eating animal foods.

Victory and Self-Mastery   *J. N. Tindall* . . . . $ 5.95
How Christ maintained a sinless character in a fallen, sinful, human nature. Facsimile Reprint.

Walking With God   *Harold Penninger* . . . . $ 7.95
God's plan provided that man could learn how to walk with Him as Enoch did before he was translated. This book gives the experiences of some of the people of the Bible who have followed in His footsteps such as Abraham, Enoch, Job, Elijah, Daniel, Peter, John and Paul.

Who Killed Candida?   *Vicki Glassburn* $17.95
Although diet is an important part of getting well, even the best food and supplements are undermined if you continue to unknowingly support yeast growth! The author will show you how making simple lifestyle choices can actually STOP THE YEAST SUPPORT CYCLE that other Candida programs do not address.

Whole Foods For Whole People   *Lucy Fuller* $10.95
Whole Foods For Whole People is not just a cookbook, but a manual to teach people how they can live a longer, healthier lifestyle by using the natural resources which surround us.

The Word Was Made Flesh   *Ralph Larson* . . . . $ 8.95
This book is on the human nature of Christ, with a limited, rather specialized objective. Dr. Larson does not deal directly with the whole issue of Christ's human nature. He traces the understanding of this aspect of Christology within the Seventh-day Adventist church from 1852–1952, providing a fairly comprehensive survey of historical data.

To order any of the above titles, see your local bookstore.

However, if you are unable to locate any title,
call 518/358-3652.